ACKNOWLEDGEMENTS

This year has been a sad ending to one era but an amazing start to a new one. I would like to dedicate this book to my mum who sadly passed away earlier this year. I know Mum, you couldn't understand how I disconnected from my creativity for so long.

It has taken 20 years to finally re-discover what I thought had disappeared forever. I was cleaning out your shed and found all my artwork and realised what had been missing from my life for so long. Mum you were always my support and hoped my life would turn around for the better one day. Well finally it has.

Many thanks Nicole for your endless support and ideas. Our spiritual connection and our destiny to meet is how my first adult colouring book has come about. I will always appreciate your encouragement, motivation and kindness. You have guided and inspired me, so my first printed book is a gift to you.

Thank you Gaynor, my spiritual marketer. You connected the purpose of my colouring book to my true purpose. You found unity where I didn't see it.

Thank you Dee for spending so much time helping me with the final details. You saw the front cover before I did.

I am full of gratitude to all my friends who have given their feedback along the way. I hope my gratitude will fill you too.

SOOTHE YOUR SOUL AND DISCOVER YOURSELF

I hope this colouring book gives your soul focus, enjoyment and freedom. Colour and creativity has helped me re-direct my sadness into happiness and has given me a sense of fulfilment and achievement.

Even if you don't possess any artistic skills, colouring is very healing and helps you tune out from everyday stress and demands which are very left brain, while colouring helps you focus on right brain creativity.

As you become absorbed in the details of the picture, you may start to feel yourself balancing and blending colours. Notice how you are feeling at the time. Are the colours you have chosen bright and happy, deep and sombre, or are they soft pastels? What mood is reflected by your colour choices?

If you find the detail of the pictures overwhelming at first, just colour something you can see clearly or something that is repetitive and let your picture evolve slowly. You will feel a sense of achievement as you start bringing your picture to life. See if you can find the hidden map of Australia on the last page.

Texta's are a great medium as you can blend two or three colours to shade or highlight areas. Don't be afraid to leave paper white to highlight where the sun hits your subject as I have done on the front cover.

These designs reflect wildlife and flora of Australia and will soothe your soul while discovering nature. There are pages to write down any thoughts or inspirations that come to you while meditating in your world of colour.

Enjoy, be peaceful and calm and give yourself permission to spend time just being creative.

TRANSFORMATION

YOUR FRAGILE WINGS TRANSCEND THE BREEZE

YOUR LIGHTNESS FLITTERS THROUGH THE TREES

THE SUN FILLED WARMTH HAS SET YOU FREE

TO BE UNIQUE, TO JUST BE ME

YOUR CREATIVE COLOURS TRANSFORMS YOUR BEING

FROM A DARK COCOON YOU'VE EMERGED SEEING

HOW THE BEAUTY OF NATURE TRANSFORMS THE SKY

FOR I HAVE BEEN BORN, A BUTTERFLY

MEDITATIONS

....
....
....
....
....
....
....
....

THOUGHTS

....
....
....
....
....
....
....
....
....
....

INSIGHTS

....
....
....
....
....
....
....
....
....

SOCIALISE

THROUGH THE LEAVES OF RAINBOW HUES

FEATHERS OF FLIGHT AWAKEN DAWN ANEW

PETALS SWAY A DANCE OF GENTLE SONG

WHILE CHATTERING A FRENZY, HERE THE PARROTS
BELONG

LADEN WITH NECTAR TASTES ARE FULFILLED

SPRING DELIVERS SWEETNESS WHILE DIFFERENCES
ARE HEALED

SHARING WITH FAMILY AND FRIENDS WHO CONFIDE

BRINGS US FULFILLMENT WHEN WE SOCIALISE

MEDITATIONS

....
....
....
....
....
....
....
....
....

THOUGHTS

....
....
....
....
....
....
....
....
....
....

INSIGHTS

....
....
....
....
....
....
....
....
....

REFLECTIONS OF ME

A LAND SO VAST YET SO UNIQUE

WHERE RED EARTH COVERS SEEDS BENEATH

SMALL LITTLE RAIN DROPS THAT BARELY
SINK THROUGH

COLOURS EMERGE INTO DRAMATIC HUE

FROM CARPETS OF EARTH SHOOTS GREEN, BLACK
AND RED

THE STURT DESSERT PEA LAY FOR MILES AHEAD

WE DON'T ALWAYS SEE BEAUTY WHEN DORMANT IN
SEED

BUT WHEN THE SEED BLOOMS, I SEE REFLECTIONS
OF ME

MEDITATIONS

....
....
....
....
....
....
....
....
....

THOUGHTS

....
....
....
....
....
....
....
....
....
....
....

INSIGHTS

....
....
....
....
....
....
....
....
....

A PLACE CALLED HOME

UP AT DAWN, THE COOL OF DAY

BEFORE DEW DROPS EVAPORATE

FROM ALL AROUND CHOIRS OF SONG

HIGHLIGHT THE MIRACLE OF THE BILLABONG

STRONG HIND LEGS REFRESHED TO BOUND

THE VAST PLAINS VOID OF WATER FOUND

PARCHED WITH HEAT FOR MILES THEY ROAM

THIS SACRED LAND, THEY CALL HOME

MEDITATIONS

....
....
....
....
....
....
....
....
....

THOUGHTS

....
....
....
....
....
....
....
....
....
....
....

INSIGHTS

....
....
....
....
....
....
....
....
....

QUIETLY

QUIETLY SLEEPING, SOFT AND GREY

INTOXIACATING EUCALYPTS PASS NIGHT TO DAY

NOTHING TOO WORRYING, A KOALAS WORLD
MOVES SLOW

MEDITATING IN NATURE FROM EARS TO TOE

BUT WAIT AN INTERRUPTION, AN OUTSIDER NEARBY

TERRITORY IS DEFENDED IN THE BLINK OF AN EYE

THE POINT HAS BEEN MADE, EVERYONE RESUMES
EATING

ONCE AGAIN, EYES CLOSING, THE EUCALYPTS
ARE A SLEEPING

MEDITATIONS

....
....
....
....
....
....
....
....
....

THOUGHTS

....
....
....
....
....
....
....
....
....
....
....

INSIGHTS

....
....
....
....
....
....
....
....

RENEWAL

DEEP INSIDE THIS BARREN PLACE

ON FIRST IMPRESSION SEEMS AN EMPTY SPACE

BUT ON THE ROCKS OF ANCIENT PAST

ARTISTIC RELICS REVEAL WISDOMS GRASP

FROM JUST A GLANCE YOU WOULDN'T KNOW

THE FIRST RAIN INVITES THE EARTH TO GROW

FROM BARREN TO HEAVEN THE EYE BEHOLDS

A NEW VISION OF PERFECTION BEFORE ME UNFOLDS

MEDITATIONS

....
....
....
....
....
....
....
....
....

THOUGHTS

....
....
....
....
....
....
....
....
....
....

INSIGHTS

....
....
....
....
....
....
....
....
....

REMEMBER TO LAUGH

THERE ARE SOME DAYS WHEN I TRY TO PRETEND

THAT EVERYTHINGS FINE, WHEN I REALLY NEEDED
A FRIEND

I PUT ON A BRAVE FACE AND TRY TO KEEP SMILING

BUT IT'S ALL I CAN DO TO STOP MYSELF CRYING

THEN, AS IF NATURE SENT THE MESSAGE
LOUD AND CLEAR

A DISTRACTION FROM NATURE TAKES ME CLOSER
TO HEAR

KOOKABURRAS LAUGHING AT THE TOP OF THEIR
VOICE

NATURES OWN SYMPHONY INVITES US TO REJOICE

MEDITATIONS

....
....
....
....
....
....
....
....
....

THOUGHTS

....
....
....
....
....
....
....
....
....
....
....

INSIGHTS

....
....
....
....
....
....
....
....
....

SHARE THE WARMTH

UPON THE ROCKS OF CROWDED SHORES

LIE BASKING IN THE SUN

A GROWLING CHOIR OF ENDLESS EYES

TO SEEK THE PERFECT ONE

THEIR LEATHER SKIN AND ROLLING NECKS

THAW FROM ICY SEAS

TO FIND A MATE TO SHARE THE WARMTH

BEFORE THE WINTER FREEZE

MEDITATIONS

....

....

....

....

....

....

....

....

THOUGHTS

....

....

....

....

....

....

....

....

....

....

INSIGHTS

....

....

....

....

....

....

....

....

FREEDOM

FREEDOM TO ROAM NO BOUNDARIES PREVAIL

GLIDING THE CURRENTS, SUCH STRENGTH IN
THEIR TAIL

POWERS THEM FORWARD TO DEPTHS OF THE SEA

THEIR SONAR DETECTING, FOES OF THE DEEP

WORKING TOGETHER IN PLAYTIME AND LIFE

UNIFIES THESE FAMILIES IN TIMES OF NEAR STRIFE

BUT SOON THEY RELAX AND SURFACE FOR AIR

A LESSON IS LEARNT FROM A FAMILY WHO CARE

MEDITATIONS

....
....
....
....
....
....
....
....
....

THOUGHTS

....
....
....
....
....
....
....
....
....
....
....

INSIGHTS

....
....
....
....
....
....
....
....
....

TIME TO LET GO

CRYSTAL CLEAR, EXPANSIVE SEAS

WAVES IN MOTION, WARM SUMMER BREEZE

TIME TO LET GO OF SELF-DEFEATING FEARS

OPEN YOUR EYES AND A NEW WORLD APPEARS

MOVING IN HARMONY, AN EFFORTLESS GLIDE

A MAGNIFICENT PARADISE AWAITS THOSE WHO TRY

LOOK AT ALL THE MAGIC LIFE CAN PROVIDE

EXPERIENCE FREEDOM, JUST FLOW WITH THE TIDE

MEDITATIONS

....
....
....
....
....
....
....
....
....

THOUGHTS

....
....
....
....
....
....
....
....
....
....
....

INSIGHTS

....
....
....
....
....
....
....
....
....

About the Author

This book is dedicated to my mother whose recent passing has brought me back to my purpose. After 20 years of losing sight of my direction and being caught up in day to day life I have rediscovered my creativity and want to celebrate this milestone with you.

I was born to draw! I completed a Fine Art Degree in drawing and set up and ran a hand painted silk business in the early 1990s, but life and earning a living got in the way of my purpose and passion.

Today wildlife, art and spirituality have once again unified me into a happier, more peaceful person. I have come full circle, this time with new meaning and purpose.

There is more to life, you just have to be prepared to ask yourself questions, search, do what it takes to find your purpose - it's worth it.

Printed by InHouse Publishing

National Library of Australia Cataloguing-in-Publication entry

Creator: Roche, Allison, author, illustrator.

Title: Soothe your soul and discover nature / Allison Roche.

ISBN: 9781925388411 (paperback)

Subjects: Coloring books--Australia.
               Color--Therapeutic use.
               Stress management.
               Creative ability.
               Nature in art.
               Wildlife art--Australia.

Dewey Number: 741.2

www.ingramcontent.com/pod-product-compliance
Lightning Source LLC
Chambersburg PA
CBHW080058280326
41934CB00014B/3351